SONGS,

BY

Jingo!

SOMETIME

A PUBLIC-SCHOOL BOY.

LONDON:

EDWARD WEST, 97, NEWGATE STREET.

TO

JACK FROST,

ON HIS UNMISTAKABLE RETURN

TO OLD ENGLAND IN

1861,

These Original Songs by

JINGO,

ARE MOST FEELINGLY

DEDICATED.

CONTENTS

———

CONTENTS

Songs, by Jingo!

SONGS, BY JINGO!

The Old English Constable.

Tune, "The Old English Gentleman."

1.

I'LL sing you of a good old boy, whom all must now revere,
Of a fine old English constable, who lived for many a year;
Who, though his natural looks were kind, could oft be most severe,
And could whene'er he had a mind strike every one with fear—
  Like a fine old English constable, one of the olden time.

2.

His office was to keep the peace and order of the town,
To take the roaming spirits up, and knock the rising down.
They wanted then no new police, with hats glazed round the crown,
To strut about, for he did all, in rare old rusty gown—
  Like a grand old English constable, one of the olden time.

3.

He often had to ring a bell, that every one might hear
When goods were stolen, strayed, or lost, in accents loud and clear;
So maidens when their reticules were miss'd, did never fear
For love letters were found before they reached the parent' ear—
  Like a good old English constable, one of the olden time.

B

4.

Each Sunday morn he stood in church with magisterial suit,
And looked like something more than man, and little less than
  brute;
And when the service had begun, and every thing was mute,
He made each little charity boy shrink into his half boot—
 Like a fierce old English constable, one of the olden time.

5.

Then he would raise his mighty staff, and fix his rolling eye,
And hit the young ones on the poll, that is upon the sly.
Poor urchins, they dared not roar out, nor yet begin to cry,
But patiently received the thump and bore it tranquilly,
 From the sly old English constable, one of the olden time.

6.

He had to keep throughout the town repose in every quarter,
And when he found a scolding wife, immediately he'd start her.
And if his phiz, which would have posed the brains of a Lavater,
Had no effect, full soon he'd show the rig he would be ar'ter—
 Like a fine old English constable, one of the olden time.

7.

He was respected and beloved by all who knew his worth,
By those who took their *wet*, when first they'd blown away the
  froth,
By old and young, by sick and strong, by all who felt his troth;
By those who drained the bowl of punch, and those the mutton
  broth—
 Like a kind old English constable, one of the olden time.

8.

But times are changed, and such old blades are getting out of date,
And each old parish constable's resigning to his fate;
Most of them have departed; ah, 'tis piteous to relate!
And few, indeed, are left behind to hold their old estate—
    Like a fine old English constable, one of the olden time.

9.

Yet, never mind, whilst one remains old England cannot fall;
And some old country town still boasts a grand original
In ancient suit, which has gone down from others great and small,
He may be found with all his staff against the old Town Hall—
    Like a grand old English constable, one of the olden time.

ENCORE VERSES.

10.

Though then no corporate reform enforced more watchful care,
And *councilmen* were things of course, and much the same the
    mayor,
He'd keep his weather eye well out, and always on the stare,
And fail not to report those who his vigilance would dare—
    Like a fine old English constable, one of the olden time.

11.

He had to keep all well behaved, not only poor, but rich,
To mind the groggy, when they fell, remain'd not in the ditch,
That is, the gutter in the street; but it does not matter which
When folks get screwy, and will all behave themselves "*as sich*"—
    Like a kind old English constable, one of the olden time.

12.

Now all you coves municipal who still keep up your tricks,
Bethink you well before you make old servants "cut their sticks."
From a good old English constable you might run away "like
    bricks,"
But now, when free you make you'll see your case become a fix
    With a fine new English constable, none of the olden time.

Returned from the Diggings.

Tune—" Guy Fawkes," or " Tow, row, row."

1.

I'm a gent again, and in the lounge of life am quite a show man,
Reported rich—and therefore I'm no longer Mr. No-Man.
The reason's plain—I'll tell it you—I'm just come off the
    diggings,
And with my pockets jolly lin'd,—oh, wouldn't some like prig-
    gings!
        And—oh, dear me !
    How old faces tumble in to ask how I be.

2.

They us'd to say, "All wasn't gold that glisten'd," but I say now,
Old maxims are quite out of date in this enlighten'd day, now.
What Sinbad saw, or Crusoe did, is really quite a failure
To all the rigs of modern prigs advent'ring in Australia.
        So—oh, dear me !
    Emigrate, at any rate, if buffers you would be.

3.

There's old aunt Ann who ever was as stiff as any rocket,
And close as wax,—although I knew she'd no end of a pocket;
Now bids me to drop in and dine, at pleasure any day where
I'll always have a seat and find them in a family way there !
        And—oh, dear me !
    Plenty's all the go when one don't want it, you see.

4.

Before I left to dig for gold I seldom was invited
To dine with family nobs, but now I am no longer slighted;
For e'er they're making spreads for me, and titled folks request-
"To honour them by meeting one so very interesting!"   [ing
       And—oh, dear me!
    How the treats accumulate when prosperous and free.

5.

"A fast young man" they thought I was, and so the dons for-
    sook me.
And some of them said, "t'would be well if pinching days o'er-
    took me."
He'd ne'er give me the least blow out; Confound it, uncle
    Horner!
Whene'er I leave my house I twig him coming round the corner!
       And—oh, dear me!
    To drop in for a "snack" at lunch, dinner, or tea.

6.

Before I went abroad to *axe* my way to get the dibs a bit,
Some used to pass me in the street as if stiff in the ribs a bit!
But "Golden ointment" now 'tis plain decreases human blind-
    ness,
So through the mud they hop to show the milk of human kind-
       And—oh, dear me!   [ness!
    How attentions wait on all when risen in degree!

7.

I us'd to sneak down Regent street, as if to friends an eyesore,
In shady suit and countenance like one of Scinde or Mysore;
Or slipp'ry fellow fallen down from some unknown creation,
The gemman in the moon perhaps, or some one in his station!
       And—oh, dear me!
    State of life, how different 'tis—when top o' the tree.

8.

Now fortune made, and made a man; they wish that I would
    shake off
The company I kept, and give some few a hint to make off;
But I will stick to them who stuck to me when hardly driven,
And by whose homely firesides the hearty fare was given!
        For—oh, dear me !
      Most of life is only show, and fiddle de dee.

9.

I'll never yield to their advice and such opinions gratis,
And turn my back on former friend however queer his state is !
And if a few who stood me true have gone where none can find
    them,
I'll give a helping hand to those in want, and left behind them—
        As, plain to me,
      Aid in time is every thing on life's wild sea.

ENCORE VERSES.
10.

When visiting I often heard-say, "call again to-morrow,"
And when admitted, most would look as if I wish'd to borrow,
But, now whene'er I call, for me, an easy chair, they set it,
And look as if *they* wish'd a loan—but, *I* wish they may get it ;
        And—oh, dear me !
      Money makes the man, you'll find, wherever you may be.

11.

A " rummy chap," they look'd on me, and not of consequence a bit,
A man when down and once done brown, has nothing, e'en not
    sense a bit.
Of ha'-pence !—oh, I us'd to get much less than rubs or kickings,
But now, such things have chang'd with me, and they've gone to
    the (*dickens*) DIGGINGS !
        And—oh, dear me !
      "Wheel about and turn about's " the fashion I see.

12.

My children dear " were brats and queer" to others left a show
    to be,
The blame they bore whilst I was poor like puss or Mr. Nobody,
But now, "they've grown *such ducks*" they own, though one's a
    a hobble-de-hoy now;
My girl a family pattern is, and Joe's a promising boy now,
      And, oh dear me!
    Nature even fluctuates with £. s. d.

13.

Now *prudent* mothers wonder how that any e'er could flout me!
And why the *gals* so quickly see gray hairs have come about me,
Whilst dearest Angeline's mamma thinks by-gones immaterial,
And dotes with her fair daughter on my moustache and imperial.
      But—oh, dear me!
    I can't marry all that set their cap *now* at me.

Meet me by Gaslight.

Tune—" Meet me by Moonlight."

1.

Meet me by gaslight alone,
And I will tell you a tale ;
'Tis to be told by the gaslight alone,
At the steps by the area rail.
Remember, be sure to be there,
When every thing's still in the street,
When there's not a breath in the air,
I'll whisper you something that's sweet.

     Then meet me by gaslight alone,
     Meet me by gaslight alone.

2.

Lamplight is now in the dark,
And darker the better, and why ?
I care not for night-lights a spark,
While I am the spark in your eye.
Then, Mary, be sure to be there,
On tiptoe, and quiet your feet ;
For should your bell ring, I declare,
'Twill be any thing, love, but a treat.

     But meet me by, &c.

3.

I'll show you how love makes his dart
So gentle, and yet so acute.
I'll tell how he teaches by heart
The tender idea how to shoot.
In the balcony over the street,
Young mistress may flirt with her beau ;
'Tis hard, then, you never may meet
Your *Jeames* by the railings below.

So meet me, &c.

4.

I'll show you how matches are made,
And lighted as soon as begun.
Of master, then, don't be afraid,
Or mistress, dear girl, or we're done.
They allow not for servants a rush ;
Such selfishness sours and galls.
They think there's no heart within plush,
No sentiment ever in smalls.

So meet me, &c.

Aunt's Lament at the use of Slang.

Tune—" Cock Robin."

1.

OH ! never did I hear the like, what is the world about ?
" I wish you now may get it"—" Does your mother know you're
Is all the go on every lip, there's scarce a decent talker ! [out ?"—
The only question's, " Who are you ?"—The answer, " Hookey
     Walker."

2.

I never meet my nephy John, and ask him " How do ye do ?"
But he says, " Aunty, you're a brick," or else, " Aunt, who are
     you ?"
Or you're a " buffer," or a " trump," tis really quite provoking,
One never knows if such young blades are serious or joking.

3.

'Tis vain attempting, in the least, with such remarks to cope,
As " cut your lucky,"—" up the spout,"—" how are you off for
     soap ?"
And if I don't forbear, and try such ugly words to smother,
It's " call again to-morrow, aunt," or else, " why you're another."

4.

I never dare interrogate the youngster, " where he's been ? "
But he begins " to blow me tight," or tell me " all's serene."
And if I venture to implore such language he'll eschew ;
Why, shut your " tater trap," he says, or, " squeeze me if I do."

5.

Oh, dear ! 'tis awful quite to think, how bad the youngster talks,
If I inquire about any thing, he bids me " walk my chalks."
My lips thus sealed, what is the use of stirring up a wrangle,
He'd only come it stronger with, " Has your mother sold her
    mangle ? "

6.

But what's the odds !—By all his jeers, his chaffing, and his
    flamming,
I suppose he thinks *weak* woman must for ever want a *cramming*.
" There you go with your eye out " may provoke one—and such
    lingo !
But with my eye remaining, I can see him through, by jingo !

7.

Old women, like old birds, cannot by chaff be taken in,
And they don't always " come it mild," when they in turn begin.
So all young gemmen ere I close, take warning by my song ;
Beware you do not " come the fool," when you try to come it
    strong.

ENCORE VERSES.

8.

I bade him once to Uncle Dick display much more regard,
'Twas due to age I said—but he said, Uncle's "quite a card."
I could not hear my brother dear compared to knave of trumps,
And so I told the youth—but he told me to "mind my stumps."

9.

I told him that behaviour such my even temper "ril'd,"
Still he show'd not the least concern, but bade me "draw it
    mild."
I then exclaimed, You can't suppose that disrespect is "mannish,"
When he rejoined, "shut up" dear Aunt, or else you'd better
    "vanish."

10.

I hinted once, he ey'd too much his cousin fair Louise,
When he replied, "Pull up your boot,—to flirt is quite the cheese."
In fact I thought he'd never stop his strange unmeaning chatter,
Which ended to my great surprise with, "Aunty, who's your
    hatter ? "

11.

If I say smoking makes the day of health too quickly fly,
He says, " When it has cook'd my goose, then you may pipe
    your eye."
Of consequences sad, though warn'd, he takes but little heed,
But tells me, " He don't care a *rush,* so that he has his *weed.*"

When my Great Aunt dies.

Tune—" Eveleen's bower."

1.

I've taken every care
To gain a proper share
Of necessary comforts from the world's supplies ;
Still luxuries I want,
And afford 'em now I can't,
But "please the pigs" I'll have 'em,

     When my great aunt dies.

2.

Then I'll put on the steam,
And what was all a dream,
When striving hard to make my boiling kettle top arise,
Will roll it on a flood
Of reality so good ;
I'll wear the deepest mourning,

     When my great aunt dies.

3.

My Kidderminster's bare,
My drugget's worse for wear,
And a Turkey or a Brussels' one would benefit sore eyes.
No closet I can boast,
Nor smoke-jack fit to roast ;
But I'll have 'em all or burn me,

     When my old aunt dies.

4.

I've a pump in my yard,
The water's very hard,
If a bottle's in my cellar found, how greatly t'will surprise ;
A bitter draught is here,
But I'll have my bitter beer,
Sherry cobbler, and my Jackey,

> When my great aunt dies.

5.

I've got no sugar-tongs,
My forks have but two prongs ;
Handy things you'll say when treated with green peas o' little
My tea pot leaks about,   [size.
And my urn has ne'er a spout,
But I'll have a change, oh ! won't I,

> When my old aunt dies.

6.

How hard and how fast
She holds on to the last.
She's tough enough for any thing, which nobody denies ;
Dame Nature's very clever,
But she can't hold on for ever,
And, oh ! what will I not do,

> When my old aunt dies.

7.

Then why not be jolly,
To fret is worse than folly.
They say in expectation 'tis real happiness lies ;
But still I'll shed a tear
For a relative so dear,
And ever dress in sable,

> When my great aunt dies.

Tom Bowling, jun.'s, lament on his return from Cronstadt.

Tune—"The Misletoe Bough."

1.

Don't ask me "old gal" why the mist's o'er my eye,
"Us sailors" have feelings, my Polly—
We know not a fear when an enemy's nigh,
And even in danger we're jolly.

So muzzle your lips, and my word never doubt it, .
'Tis well my poor father knows nothing about it !

2.

You've heard, Poll, of father, " Tom Bowling" of yore ;
There's nothing that he was afraid of :
He's gone up aloft ! but he can't be no more,
For his country knows what he was made of,

The thought of our flinching at stone walls, he'd scout it !
'Tis well the brave fellow knows nothing about it !

3.

'Twas then that old England had rule o'er the sea,
And nought could escape from her cruisers,
But now, to speak plain like a Briton that's free,
We have not the same " Harry-thusers !"   (Arethusas.)

Oh, arn't this enough, Poll, to make a chap flout it!
'Tis well my old father knows nothing about it.

4.

Says he in the very last yarn that he spun,
(Soon after his death bell was tolling)
" If enemies show and you ne'er fire a gun,"
" You're never a chip of Tom Bowling."

To Cronstadt I've been, Poll ;—no wonder you doubt it,
And well 'tis poor father knows nothing about it !

5.

Great Nelson had never such ships in his day,
Our guns carry double as far now !
To think then that *Rooshians* should keep us at bay,
I'm blowed if I'm son of a tar now !

A land-lubber, Polly ! though well you may doubt it,
And well too poor father knows nothing about it.

6.

Oh ! shiver my mizen, this half and half game
Must damage Britannia's glory,
To think that a lion a bear couldn't tame;
'Twill look rather rummy in story.

Than this, oh, I'd sooner my bacca-box spout it !
And well 'tis poor father knows nothing about it.

Going to the Camp.

Tune—" Hunting the Hare."

1.

JOEY, my dear, arise,
Open those precious eyes,
Quickly each moment flies:
        Out is the lamp.

Bright is the peep of day,
Lovey, make no delay!
Trains won't a moment stay,
        Bound for the camp.

All are for Waterloo,
From ev'ry quarter too!
Here's your hot water—do
        Shave that dear face

Pack'd are the mutton pies,
All such a jolly size!
Nobody now denies
        Chobham's the place.

(*Spoken.*) We shall never be in time, Joe! its hagra*w*ating—I say its hagra*w*ating. All right, Martha? Yes, love; but I'm not going to be dragg'd as if I was no better than I hought to be, and have my best Bal*serene* all shreds and patches, like "'Amlet's" ghost on the *platform*. Well, Martha, my dear, I'm up, and in five minutes we shall—both

(*Chorus.*)   Slash away,
           Dash away—
           With the world flash away,
           There'll be a crash to-day
                Down at the camp.

C

2.

Now they soon make a start,
Both with a merry heart,
Anxious to play a part
            In the day's fun.

Look for a cabby to
Take them to Waterloo;
But there is none in view,
            So they must run!

Then at the ticket place—
Wife in a shocking case!
Red is her melting face—
            Mellow as cheese.

Arms at the socket sore,
Dress at the pocket tore,
Purse and a locket bore
            Off in the squeeze!

(*Spoken.*) What con*traries* do we meet with to be sure!
Here we goes, Joe, for a sham fight from Waterloo—where,
before, they ended with a real one, and no mistake. What's
the odds, Martha, so long as " yer happy?" Law, Joe, what a
ciwilian you be! you talks more 'orred than a " *queerasssheer.*"
(*Joey aside*). One of her old grannydeers, I suppose. Never
mind, Martha, but—

(*Chorus.*)   Slash away, dash away, &c.

3.

Tickets produc'd, and right—
For a seat have a fight!
Joe in a sorry plight,
      Bung'd in the eye,

Livid and spherical—
Martha hysterical,
Not much a merry gal,
      Off as they fly.

Lots of companions rough—
Weeds smoking quite a puff.
Is it not, Joe, enough
      To drive one mad?

Rise, dear, upon your legs.
Can't, love; they're jamm'd like pegs.
You're sitting on the eggs,
      Joe, it's too bad!

(*Spoken*). Guard, I say, guard! we're six full-siz'd ones all in a row; and I'll thank you to lift *these here eggs* from underneath my Joe. Arn't no business of mine, marm; nothing to do with eggs. Will you do me the favour, sir, to relieve my husband from his embarrassments? Wery 'appy to do any neighbour a turn, marm; but you see I've only one '*and*, and the tother has been trying to scrape an acquaintance with my bird's eye wipe the last half hour; but they be as far off each other as you be from Hamster*dam*. What language!! but it's—

(*Chorus*). Slash away, dash away, &c.

4.

'Tis but a spurt; the two
Staines reach, and Chertsey too!
Martha makes curtsies to
          Cad of a bus.

When woman's in the case
Ev'ry thing else gives place;
Cad, with approving face,
          Gives her a push!

" Bang " goes the door, and smack
Goes the whip—off they crack—
Where's Martha ?—on her back!
          Stunning her kicks—

Footing she cannot find—
Conductor doesn't mind.
Where's Joey ? left behind.
          Lawk, what a fix!

(*Spoken*).   Will you get up, marm ?   Your parasol has nearly extracted my eye from its socket. And your " humberrella," sir, has so contracted me that I can't support myself *were* it never so! Here we are! Here's the Encampment! here's Chobham! Will you get up, old woman? I say, Pa, which be the Life Guards? I know which be the blackguards, my dear, to let a hunprotected female be bundled into a bus this here way, and no deliverance.   Yes, marm, and to have the centre of the wehicle stopped up like Lowther Harcade in an 'ail-storm. Conductor! turn that fat talkative gentleman hout. Not so easy, marm, if you please, with nine heach side, and five bodkins ! Rolling pins you ought to say.   Never mind, but—

(*Chorus*).   Slash away, dash away, &c.

5.

Camp reach'd and battle plain,
Bus at a stand again—
All try to quit in vain,
        Such is the jam.

Cannonade just begun,
Out they come one by one—
Martha quite flat and done,
        Nothing of sham!

For attack, trumpets sound,
Troops advance o'er the ground,
Volleys discharg'd around;
        Form in a square

Soldiers are trying to,
Spectators flying too,
Many ones eyeing too
        Highlanders bare!

(*Spoken*). Well, I'll never come no more! I am a lone woman, and Joe a lost indiwidual—that he should have left me as he 'ave done! Pray, marm, are you the lady wot has lost her tother part? I've lost my dearly beloved, sir. Exactly so, marm; and there's a strange gentleman run down by one of the Dragons, and nobody 'll own him. Had he a black heye, sir? Don't know, marm; but he'd a red nose, and two teeth hout. Then it's Joey!

(*Chorus*).   So dash away, crash away,
              Bad news will flash away;
              O what a smash to-day
                    Down at the Camp!

6.

Gain'd is the wictory O !
Chas'd are the beaten foe !
Oh ! if there isn't Joe
                    Flying in front !

Martha screams shrill and clear,
Spare my lost Hubby dear :
If again he comes here
                    Surely I *wunt!*

Once with him met again,
Steps are home set again ;
Down comes the wet again,
                    Walking to Staines.

Martha fagg'd, fit to fall,
Thinks they've had ar'ter all,
Nothing to pleasure call
                    For all their pains.

(*Spoken*). No, Joey; I'll never go no more to Camps, that I won't—it's *hawful!* Why you're not so knock'd up neither, Martha, as you fancy. Fancy, Joe ! why I'm beaten to a jelly, and I'm all over no how. Goodness gracious ! a pretty time o' night, too ! what says your ticker, Joe ? Why—hum—hah—. Oh ! what you ar'n't lost the family turnip ? No, love, not exactly; it's only wegetating at Chobham. Then it's gone, Joe ? Yes, love; fell in the retreat—chances of war. Oh, Joe! that turnip was—. Stop, love; it's no use a running on, may be it's *cabbaged!* Well, I'll have no more Camps—no, we wont, dear—not no more—but—

(*Chorus*).   Stay at home, keep at home,
                Patterns be then to some—
                Blow'd if I ever come
                    More to a Camp !

The Lost Boy at the Exhibition, 1851.

A MEDLEY.

Tune—" Blue Bells of Scotland."

Oh ! where and O where can my precious darling be !
In glass, *all in glass*, yet my way I cannot see ;
But, oh ! *at last*, a Peeler-man—a Peeler-man is near !
He shall know all my woe, and may find my wandering dear.

Tune—" Pray Goody."

Policeman, have you seen my boy ? My little darling duck !
We have come from Ponder's End this very day,
You must have seen him—such a dear ! at breakfast he did tuck,
You'd have thought that he could never run away.
   You, sir ! Do, sir !
  Search the building through, sir.
A father's ruby veins I'm sure
Flow 'neath that coat of blue, sir !
Oh ! no, indeed, I am not, marm, a family man, and so
To the Telegraph electric you must go.
   You, sir ! Do, sir !
  Search the building through, sir.

A father's ruby veins I'm sure
Flow 'neath that coat of blue, sir !
Oh ! no, indeed, I am not, marm, a family man, and so
To the Telegraph electric you must go.
   You, sir ! Do, sir !
  Search the building through, sir.

Air—" Non più andrai."

Don't cry and give way to your woe so,
He's safe, marm! and soon you shall know so!
But describe him from top to the toe so—
We may know 'mongst the lot to look for,
But describe him from top to the toe so—
We may know 'mongst the lot to look for.

Air—" Monument and St. Paul's."

Lost, or stray'd, or gone off afraid
At the sight of this Great Exhibition,
A fine little boy, his mammy's joy,
  Who he's left in a terrible condition!
(Sobbing.) He stands three feet nuffing (nothing),
And does not want stuffing!
I'm not given to starve my dear children,
I'm no Mrs. Sloane, or dealer in bone,
But I'm all over maz'd and bewild'ring.
His hair's light brown, rather stiff at the crown!
His nose has a turning up—rather!
His dear fat cheeks, whenever he speaks,
Has a smile like his excellent father!
He's timid and shy, with a sty in each eye,
But they're all very well in the socket.
But now to be brief, he's a pockethand'chief
And a tartlet in his right breeches pocket.
Then set the telegraph to work, right, left, and up and down,
And bring to his disconsolate ma! Young Master Abr'am Brown!

Oh! dear, dear me! I scarce can see,
My mind! My poor mind so distress'd is,
P'liceman, you're good, but you've ne'er understood,
What a pang in a fond mother's breast is!
But, oh! to proceed, he's a little knock-knee'd,
Though it hardly would meet your detection,

His ears are turn'd flat by the brim of his hat,
But then he's a lovely complexion ;
His jacket is blue, and almost bran new !
His trousers are piec'd at the feet, sir,
But they are not bad for a fine growing lad,
Tho' patch'd a small bit 'bout the seat, sir !
And tho' I says it that should'nt, I know he would'nt
Touch a thing, my dear sir, that war'nt his 'n ;
So I know he's at large, and never in charge
For any thing that may be " miss'n."
So now then for you enough I've gone through,
Of his form, of his dress, and his feature.
And this I'm pos—there never once was
A more innocent, tractable creature !
Then set the telegraph to work, right, left, and up and down,
And bring to his disconsolate ma ! Young Master Abr'am Brown !

Recit.

With magic speed at sight of silvery crown !
The wires are work'd to find the missing Brown.
And, lo ! where Nature smiles through chasten'd art,
A youth is spied—and with a raspberry tart !
The *naked* truth thus very soon comes out !
Oh ! Master Brown, what are you boy about !

Air—" Lullaby."

Softly gazing, lost in wonder !
Innocently sitting down !
By the Greek Slave's influence yonder !
See reposing—Master Brown.
Fol-de-dol-Tid-i-Dol !
Fol-de-dol-Tid-i-dol !
Who'd have thought it, Master Brown !

Tune—"British Grenadiers."

By Peeler B the boy's then led
By his brim-turnèd ears
To his distracted fountain-head,
O'erwhelmèd with her tears.
The urchin's squall astoundeth all
The building with its noise;
Which then she quits, consid'ring it's
No place for little boys!

Tune—From Song, " Elfin call—Come away Elves."

Come along, boy ?   You've shock'd me through !
Catch me a sight-seeing 'gain with you.
Here, policeman ! Here's your due—
                 One bob !
    Come, come away !
    Come, come away ! Come, come away !
    Come ! Come away !

The "Fancy Fair."

SONG OF THE SHOWMAN.

Tune—" Soho Bazaar."

1.

LADIES and Gents—come to our tents,
Stalls are all ready, so do now
  Humour your taste,
  Ev'ry thing chaste
Is *fairly* presented to you now.
(*Chorus.*)   Here's the Bazaar—foremost by far!
  Sing "diddle diddle, three cheers and huzza!"
  Here's the Bazaar—foremost by far!
  Sing "diddle diddle, three cheers and huzza!"

2.

That in Soho, long all the go,
Or the Pantheon so famous,
  If to this ère
  You match, why compare
A mouse to a hippo*tamus*!
  Chorus, &c.

3.

Come and "buy, buy," that which your eye,
Your whim, your wants, or your fancy
    First may entice,
    Don't think about twice,
Hesitation should none in a man see!
          Chorus, &c.

4.

Articles here mingled appear,
Useful as they're ornamental!
    Baby things good,
    Dolls as they should
Be *dress'd* to please feelings parental.
          Chorus, &c.

5.

Finely spun hose, silks for the nose,
Or neck, in variety see now!
    Robes and corsets,
    Nicknacks for pets—
So pray let your purse-strings go free now!
          Chorus, &c.

6.

Here are soft shoes for gout in the toes,
Uglies so blue and so shady!
    Here's a *fur* cap
    For a cool-headed chap—
And here's crinoline for his lady!
          Chorus, &c.

7.

Case for cigars—family jars!
Housewives for bachelor *naturs!*
    Furniture rare
    For new-married pair—
Doubling-up *perambulators!*
        Chorus, &c.

8.

Choice table mats, toys for your brats,
Presents of ev'ry invention—
    Scent bottles full,
    Garters of wool!
Things far too many to mention.
        Chorus, &c.

9.

Haste, then, and sport, cash you have brought,
Your notes, your silver and gold now.
    Think of the cause,
    That freely draws,
All friends to the Fair which we hold now.
(*Chorus.*)   Here's the bazaar—foremost by far!
    No diddle diddle—three cheers and huzza!

Romeo and Juliet.

A MEDLEY.

Recit.

I sing a song, but ere I move a stave,
Your patience and indulgenee I must crave ;
For though 'tis new, the tale in days of old
Was by the Bard of lucid Avon told !
The greatest *Bill* Apollo drew upon
The Muses' Bank (*Joint Stock*) at Helicon !
Where Fame presides, and through whose fadeless source,
The draft for ever honour'd is—of course ;
And throughout time no Bill can e'er be greater !
Ah ! William Shakspere, you knew a *leetle* bit of *human natur !*

Air—" Ratcatcher's Daughter."

Once on a time in Italy,
And not a lie you'll find it,
Two heads of houses had a " shy,"
But the young 'uns didn't mind it :
For Romeo, heir to Montague,
In love lost his digestion
With Cap'let's daughter, pretty Ju !
So he popp'd to her the question.
          Doodle dum, doodle di, dum di diddle Pa !

Air—" A frog he would a wooing go."

Then Romy would a wooing go,
    " O dear ! " cries Romy.
Poor Romy would a wooing go,
And he felt very queer, as most of us know,
    With a family scrimmage,
    All gammon and spinach,
    Heigh ho ! for Montague Romy !

His love was fairest of the fair
    In that gay quarter.
All ladies are fair, as you all are aware,
Whether brown in the eye, the skin or the hair,
    Or a darkee like jet,
    Or a pretty brunette,
And fair was Capulet's daughter.

Recit.

Poor Juliet ! 'tis no wonder Romeo won her,
And love should *weigh* him down, she was a *stunner !*

Air—" Darby Kelly."

And, lack-a-day ! it fell one night,
When mother Capulet did invite
Verona's gayest belles and beaux,
With faces mask'd and dominoes,
To shake their youthful pettitoes,
That Romeo went—but how ?—none knew !
For as he was a Montague,
And any thing besides a chum,
He was not ask'd, of course, to come
To Madame Capulet's blow out
Or rout—
(Spoken.) The fact is, he went without.

(SUNG.) And hence it was that he did get
      But few sweet looks with Juliet,
      That once for all his heart upset,
      And tangled him up in the net
      That Cupid weaves up in a minute !
      Cobwebs are fools to it !—don't get in it !

Air—" We won't go home till morning."

    For you won't get out so easy !
      You won't get out so easy !
      You won't get out so easy !
        At least without a fuss !

Air—" Cock Robin's Courtship.'

A tête-à-tête the fond ones had,
    'Twas very short and sweet !
But all oppos'd to Mam and Dad,
    Their woes were soon complete.
For Mammy rav'd, and Daddy swore
    The match should never be—
Which made the gallant Sposo more
    Determined to have she !

Oh ! governors ! you've flinty hearts
    Who pose young Nature thus !
Forgetting quite, that true love starts
    As certain as a *bus!*
But now, to cut a long tale short,
    Between these tender spouses
A cruel fate soon spoilt their sport,
    " A plague on both their houses !"

For, oh ! the gay Mercutio
    Embroil'd with Tybalt gets,
And whips him off at once unto
    The tomb of Capulets.

Thus soon as had these true loves been
   Tied up in marriage bond
Was Romy sent, for change of scene,
   Across the " herring pond."

Air—"Auld Robin Gray."

Then 'twas that Juliet ran
   To Friar Lawrence' cell,
Resolv'd with her dear man
   In banishment to dwell,
He gave a dose to Ju !
   'Twas safe her grief to quell ;
Of love he little knew !
   But human nature well.

Tune—" There is nae luck."

A draught he order'd going to bed,
   Her senses to compose,
Which tho' 'twould make her seem as dead,
   'Twould only be a doze.
But Romy thought the news was true
   That she was dead indeed,
So ere he sought a last long view,
   He hurried off in speed

To find apothecary's aid,
   And soon, by hook and crook,
He found a chap for mischief made,
   Of lean and hungry look.

Air—"Old English Gentleman."

Then prussic acid, laud'num, but—it does not matter which,
Poor Romy purchas'd like a goose, and gobbled down as sich !
And off he went to Juliet's bier to take a last long view,
Of the little woman he had lov'd, lost Mrs. Montague,
   Like a nice young constant *lovier*,
   A pattern in his way.

She waking, rav'd, and tore her hair—her " better half " his wig,
When Juliet, lo ! a little phial very soon did twig,
The potent drug soon did its worst on Romeo—no more
His little woman said, but tried " the mixture as before."
      Like a faithful darling, every inch
      Trump, of the female kind !

Air—"Malbrook."

Sold again ! Not a drop's in the bottle !
Poor girl ! disappointed her throttle—
But now, just to *sum* up "the *tottle !*"
      She stabb'd herself right well,
      And so the fond ones fell,
      O lawk ! what a terrible sell :
And p'raps now at the theātre,
The story of which I'm narrator—
You may see enacted like *natur !*
      How Romy and July fell.

Air—" All Good Lasses."

So here's a health to all true loviers !
Here's success to all true loviers !
Here's good luck to all true loviers !
Tender chicks, and ducks, and ploviers !
      There is nought like constancy !
      Though they say, " 'Tis all my eye,"
      Though they say, " 'Tis all my eye."
      O yes !—O yes !—O yes !
      Yes !—Yes !—Yes !

Tom.

Tune—" Derry down."

1.

Some few years ago, when I first drew my breath,
My mammy and daddy were puzzled to death
To give me a name not so common as some—
Yet somehow or other they " dubb'd " me with *Tom*.
        So Tom's my name now
        Tom's my name now—
    Tom's my name—and a better can't be.

2.

Though a plain monosyllable—always " by Gom !"
I have boasted in having a sneaking for Tom—
And ask every mother's unprejudic'd son,
If he e'er knew a nobler than Tom ? he'll say none.
                So Tom's my name now, &c.

3.

Then oft as I'm thinking—and thinking admire
My many fam'd namesakes, my pride rises higher—
Names written in permanent records of fame !
There's after all something, thinks I, in a name.
                So Tom's my name now, &c.

4.

In proof of the fact I will name you a few
Of Toms who've been noted as life they pass'd through.
And first, who would dare the wreath to take from
The spirited brow of our social " Old Tom !"
                So Tom's my name now, &c.

D 2

5.

" Tom Trot " of our childhood, I call from my stock,
Companion of bulls'-eyes and peppermint rock !
And long as old England can keep what she's got,
An attachment there always must be for " Tom Trot."
                    So Tom's the name now, &c.

6.

Tom Thumb next, brave hero ! I must not let pass,
Whom a cow gobbled up in a mouthful of grass—
His body was found—and his life was not spent,
Though he did not return the same way that he went.
                    So Tom's my name now, &c.

7.

I need not tell how he was saved to the full,
But the tale, be assur'd it is no " cock and bull."
It happen'd of old, and it's ne'er been denied,
Tom left not a *stain* on his *name* when he died.
                    So Tom's the name now, &c.

8.

Next comes, and a host of queer Tommies he'll cover
On land, though he often was half the seas over !
Tom Bowling ! who rose on the pinions of fame
To a point none arrive at without a good name.
                    So Tom's my name now, &c.

9.

And last, though not least, in my catalogue's string,
There's great Tom of Oxford, the first in the ring,
Go once within sound of his stunning "Bom—Bom,"
And you ne'er will forget you have heard of " Old Tom."
                    So Tom's the name now, &c.

10.

I feel I for ever could add to the pack,
And sing to the praise of them " *ev'ry man Jack;* "
But all will allow, e'en from what has been stated,
That Tom has not heretofore been overrated!
    So Tom's my name now,
    Tom's my name now,
   Tom's my name, and a better can't be.

ENCORE VERSES.

11.

Tom Oliver—Belcher—and Cribb in their day—
Rare fellows to polish one off in a fray!
Tom Spring—and Tom Sayers, who well did employ
His fists when he fought the Benicia Boy.
     So Tom's the name now, &c.

12.

Of Coventry, fam'd peeping Tom I must hint at,
Who through a sly window did wickedly squint at
A lady of rank as she rode through the street—
With no inexpressibles on—what a treat!
     So Tom's the name now, &c.

13.

Tom saw her, and thought it a strange exhibition,
To see a fine lady in such a position—
He'd heard that sweet woman the high horse could straddle,
But he'd ne'er seen a naked one sit on a saddle.
    But Tom's the name then,
    Tom's the name then,
   Tom's the name, and a better can't be.

Gog and Magog's Duet on "City Reform."

Tune—"Garry Owen."

1.

Magog.—Dearest Gog be assur'd there's a regular fix,
　　　But I'm happy to say, *We* shall soon "cut our sticks,"
　　　For to speak the plain truth, I do really feel small,
　　　In passing through life like a brick in a wall.
　　　　　And as eggs be eggs
　　　　　I'm stiff in the legs,
　　　　　A standing upright
　　　　　By day and night !
　　　　　But City reform
　　　　　Will make a chap warm,
　　With a wheel about, turn about, weathercock storm !

2.

Gog.—Brother Magog you're right, and as I'm " *City*-vate"
　　　I'm blow'd if I care for an alderman's fate !
　　　Inquiry will throw in confusion the troop,
　　　And bother their taste for green fat in the soup.
　　　　　Full long's the year
　　　　　We've stood up here,
　　　　　A twigging below
　　　　　The wond'rous show,
　　　　　And licking in vain
　　　　　Our lips for Champagne,
　　Whilst many got more than their wits could contain.

3.

Magog.—Let others then boast of their suff'rings, dear Gog,
  Privations through life, as they fish'd for their prog—
  But where self-denial like ours can they see?
  Temptation so great, and yet "stick as we be?"
    When rare delights
    On gala nights,
    A sight supplies
    For longing eyes,
    When fair ones show
    In bodices low—
 And it's " Lo! and behold!" as we very well know!

4.

Gog.—'Tis surely then time that reform should at last
  Reward our endurance for centuries past—
  Permitted no part in the annual show,
  But fumes which ascend from the banquet below.
    No chance for Gog
    Of lush or prog,
    Or nob of wealth
    To drink his health;
    No chance to declare,
    " How hard he found there
 Fit words to respond to the toast from the chair."

5.

Magog.—No wonder the nobs are afraid of a fall,
  For a lost *corporation* must make one *feel* small!
  So I'll " cut my lucky " when once on the floor,
  And squeeze a way out, if I can, through the door.
    For as eggs be eggs
    I'm cramp'd in the legs;

But once set free
We'll have our spree—
But ere our fun
In earnest's begun
We'll get "newly rigg'd " by old Moses and Son !

6.

Both.—Then bear it with patience a little time more,
Though to bear it like puss in the corner's a bore;
And the very same corner, too, day after day,
It's enough to turn toughest of natures to clay !
'Twas bad in truth
In warmth of youth—
But now, grown old,
It keeps one cold;
But City reform
Our jackets will warm !
With its wheel about, turn 'em out, weathercock storm.
And as eggs be eggs,
We're stiff in the legs,
A standing upright
By day and night !
But City reform
Will make a chap warm,
With its wheel about, turn 'em out, weathercock storm.

ENCORE VERSES.

7.

Both.—See councilman Pekin is looking quite ill—
As *green* as a pea, yet as *blue* as a pill!

Whilst alderman Jelly thinks none should inquire
Why ven'son should smell when it comes from the fire!
  The ancient crew
  In fearful stew—
  Curtail'd of soup
  Must pine and droop!—
  And 'drift and free
  Like wrecks all at sea
On the troublesome waves of transition must be!

8.

See, many look pale as if scar'd by a ghost,
Or as if the *latch-key* of their *ward* had been lost!
Whilst alderman Stocks looks flat with surprise
At a *fall* of their glory instead of a *rise*.
  He must look done,
  To think his fun,
  And civic state
  Grows out of date—
  That ne'er in lace
  The street he may trace
Of the beadle a marching before the mace!

9.

Gog.—What " a sell " for the buffers in armour of brass
  And of steel ne'er again through the city to pass;
  None the flunkies in lace and cock'd hats to admire,
  Who'll grieve at the loss?—why the old City *Crier!*
    But as eggs be eggs,
    When free in the legs
    We'll see each sight
    By day and night.
    Blow'd if I care
    Who's made a Lord Mayor,
  Or whether there's any to fill up his chair!

10.

Magog.—Oh, think! when the Parliament houses we reach,
And hear Bright deliver himself of a speech!
And see Johnny Russell, we've heard at Guildhall
Was top of the poll, as we stood on the wall!
   Then as eggs be eggs,
   Quite free in the legs,
   To Baker Street
   We'll turn our feet.
   For at the show
   Of Madame Tussaud
Our late city friends we may see in a row.

11.

Both.—Only fancy the looks of the Peelers in blue
As we, arm in arm, first appear to their view—
Perhaps they may take us for runaway guys,
And if they should dodge us we'll bonnet their eyes!
   They'll find it hard
   To Scotland yard
   To beat retreat
   From our long feet.
   And if we knock up—
   Where is the lock-up
They can find that we shall not too fully block up?
   Then as eggs be eggs,
   Though stiff in the legs,
   We'll soon be free,
   And off with glee
   When City reform
   Will make all feel warm
With its wheel about, turn 'em out, weathercock storm.

Song

between a French Soldier and one of the 6th Dragoons, on its being proposed that the English cavalry should pass through France *en route* to the Crimea.

Tune—" The Cannibal Islands."

1.

F.—Monsieur Anglais
    You're welcome, pray
    Prolong your stay.
    In friendly way
    Embrace you us
    With hearty bus !
    And voulez vous parler français ?
    Sair, voulez vous ?
    Me friend of Blue !
B.—What fraternize ?
    Lawk ! bless your eyes—
    If kiss'd by you
    My old gal Sue
    Would soon lead me a dance—eh !
    Indeed, Mountseer,
    Your welcome here,
    Like bitter beer,
    My heart doth cheer.
F.—I've only, Sair,
    Vin ordinaire.
B.—You're a brick, my parlez vous français.

2.

F. Me go wid you,
    Me friend of Blue,
    To trash dis Roos
    For his abuse—
    I could not choose
    One for my use
B. Like jolly roast beef for your chum now?
F. Me chum! what's dat?
B. Though round my hat
    Each rifle pops
    As thick as hops—
F. Him going to dance?
B. Oui;—bang through France
    To muffle Nick and his drum now!
F. Mon cher ami?
B. No *chair* for me—
    We rest not still
    While there's a mill.
    I'll take my share
    Of ordinaire;
    You're a trump of a parlez vous chum now.

3.

F. Von Tromp call me?
    Me no can see,
    Me non comprend
    Me fren' so fond
    One Tromp one Dutch
    Me am not such—
    Dis no Rotterdam, Monsieur Blue now.
B. Hark! trumpets plain—
F. Ah! Von Tromp again!
B. Sound the advance
    To march through France.

F. Me ride all through
   De vay wid you
   On me horse chestnut, my Blue now.
B. You're devilish kind,
   Mountseer, I find—
F. He talk, by gar,
   Like *man of war!*
B. Takes me for a ship
   This rummy chip
   Of a block of a queer parlez vous now.

4.

No love so new
Was half so true,
Or quicker grew.
Between the two—
It grew so fast,
They hug at last—
John Bull and the parlez vous français.
No darling Sue
Was there to see
Her own true Blue
Kiss aught but she.
For oh ! 'twould try
Her jealous eye
To twig the fashion of France, eh !
As on they went,
The compliment
They paid outright,
How each could fight,
And each claim'd too
His Waterloo—
John Bull and the parlez vous français.

5.

So off they go
To meet the foe—
Old England true
To parlez vous—
Old enemies,
But now more wise—
No friends ever better before too !
Vin ordinaire
Will keep off care,
And English grub
Will help to drub
Old Nick ; and he
Shall plainly see
A dig in the ribs is a bore too !
Then may success
The efforts bless
Of French alliance,
English science,
And make Nick ax
Full soon for *pax,*
On marrow-bones bended and sore too !

F. Then, dear Anglais,
I beg you, pray
Prolong your stay
In friendly way !
Embrace you us
Wid hearty bus,
And learn to parler français.

Going to the Naval Review.

Tune—" Hunting the Hare."

1.

Up by four o'clock,
Wind by weathercock
East, and inspiring as grog " cold without."
Bundle up, Hubby, straight
Out of bed—or we're late.
Quickly now decorate, spite of the gout,
Already town's alive,
Rattling away they drive,
Cabbies and busses—lawk ! what shall I do ?
Betty won't stir her stumps.
Babby's down with the mumps,
Just so misfortune plumps—at a review !

SPOKEN. (Old Lady.) Now, cabby, we're all little 'uns !—Jump in my dears. Where's the prog ?—Hard bil'd eggs—pork pies —tartlets and gingerbread ! Doublestout—ginger-pop and spruce ! Something substantial, that's my way of doing business. Where's father ? Where's my old man ? Lor, Sammy ! how ansome you does look, to be sure ! I suppose, cabby, your os knows his road to Waterloo ! He knows what he's 'arter well enough, marm, and what's arter *he* sometimes—so look alive, old lady ! Now, father, you take Halbert and Harthur on your knee, and I'll ave Wictoria Halice, Hemily, Sarah Jane and the prog basket in my lap. Goodness gracious ! Why, Sam, you've gone and put your *new* crutch on my *old* corn ! Never mind, Sally, bring yourself to an anchor, and lets make a start of it ! Bless his art ! and if there isn't Bobby at the winder screaming like anythink, ho ! oh ! let me hout, let me hout, I say, if he is'nt a choking of his self with his " tops and bottoms."

Just so misfortune plumps !
Babbies will have the mumps !
Sally don't take the dumps
                    To the review.

2.

Confusion—confounded,
The station surrounded,
High and low jolly mixed up in a crowd.
Carriages rushing at,
Passengers pushing at,
Roughs, others crushing at, swearing aloud !
Bedlam was nothing to't
When the train off did shoot,
Snorting and hissing, the devil to pay !
Banish'd soon were our fears
Finding seats with our dears !
Sam and his Sal in a family way.

SPOKEN. (Old Lady.)   Here we are, here's Portsmouth, here's
Spithead.   How can you run on so, Sal !   It's only Woking !
There's the *seminary*.—The what ! Mr. Hopkins ! Pleasant place
for a break down.   (Cheerful traveller.) " Down among the dead
men."   (Another.) " Who's for a song ?

              " There she lay all that day
                    In the Bay
                    Of Biscay, oh ! "

(Old Lady.) Sammy, love ! Is there any fear of a haccident !
My art's a going like a good un ! Well I never ! Twelve o'clock
and the review to begin at ten.   If this isn't a fix I don't know
what hisn't—just like them railroad directors, tell lies like
'ailstones !

              Stop, love, don't fuss and stew,
              We'll get the journey through,
              If not, why ! *say*, that you
                    Saw the review !

3.

Obstacles gone and past—
Journey's end come at last!
All at the station fast, fuss and fume out—
Parties soon separate,
Off for the water straight,
Time, " there is none to wait,"—cannons boom out—
O then to get afloat
By steam, or other boat,
There's not a chance remote,—Lawk, what a do!
At length they find a craft
(Overcramm'd fore and aft)
Sam and his wife and the family crew.

SPOKEN.—(*Old Lady.*) Will you, my dear Sir, tell me which is the Review? Why, marm, I'm not hexpert at hexplaining hany think ; but as you may say this here is the Review—and *she's* the " Prince Halbert " with a round *starn* breaking through the smoke—and she's the " Wictory " a following of Her. (*Old Lady.*) What's wictory a woman! well, I never! (*Small child.*) Ma! I sees nothink but smoke. (*Old Lady.*) Wait a bit, love.— Goodness gracious, what a noise, too! (*Familiar Neighbour.*) That's the " Lord Hexmouth " a blowing her sides out. Isn't it jolly! Fancy yourself at an engagement, old lady. (*Old Lady.*) Don't talk to me in that way, Mr. Himp'rence ; I never knew any engagement but with my dear Sammy. I came to see a Review. Well, you sees it! I sees nothink! Well, then, I can't show you nothink! (*Old Lady to another Neighbour.*) Will you, my dear Sir, point out Spithead? Why, ma'm, it's hard to say exactly where it is, and there's such a confounded smoke. (*Old Lady.*) Ah! there it is again, nothink but smoke! (*Gent.*) Well, ma'am that black spot's Spithead. (*Old Lady.*) Well, I am greatly disappointed, not to say disgusted! Why the Waithman obelisk in Blackfriars is a king to it! (*Great commotion on board.*)

E

Ah, here they come!—here they be!—no! they harn't—they're
foul of a buoy! (*Old Lady.*) What! you don't mean to say
there's a boy in the water! (*Familiar Neighbour.*) Why, of
course there be! How d'ye suppose there'd ever be *men*-of-war
afloat if there was no *boys* there first—d'ye see!—ha! ha! ha!
(*Old Lady.*) No! I sees nothink but smoke—well, never mind.
Here's the 'Ouse of Commons in the "Perseverance," and arn't
they jolly just—look as if they were used to smoke. (*Sharp
Neighbour.*) I believe' ye, my pippin!—and grub, too, by the look
on 'em! (*Familiar Friend.*) Ay, they takes care of the *Con-
stitution!*

So what a do! squeezing through
Smoke fit to smother you!
Who'd take the trouble to see a Review!

4.

Now no more cannons roar,
All is o'er—for the shore ;
Steamers, and boats, and craft bustle away.
Quickly the smoke doth go,
Leaving a gallant show—
Walls of old England in mighty array!
Yards mann'd by British tars,
Fearless of foes or scars,
Whilst the "Queen"—bless her heart—steers her course
Cheers from her subjects free   [through—
Ring o'er the tranquil sea—
Say, then, who would not see such a *Review!*

The Costermonger's 'Prentice.

Tune—" The Ratcatcher's Daughter."

1.

You ask me how I gets my grub, and I'll keep you no longer,
I'm 'prentice to that rare old cub, " Black Joe," the costermonger.
But he's not quite as dark as night, yet something like a monkey,
And if ye doubt what I sings out, why only ax my donkey !
          Ned, come up, Ned, gee vo !
          Neddy, come up—gee vo !

2.

I lives with he of temper harsh, like others in his quarter,
His crib is where they call'd the " Marsh," but now 'tis bricks
          and mortar ;
The Board of Health for all its wealth found there a nice in-
          westment,
But their queer game I mind the same as the Hincome Tax Has-
          sessment !
          Ned, &c., &c., &c.

3.

I rise at five as I'm alive, tho' half dead every morning !
Yet as for rest I'm ne'er undress'd, I takes no time adorning !
And then I turn my steps to earn a *bob* from cook or flunkey,
But if ye doubt my whereabout—inwestigate my donkey !
          Ned, &c., &c., &c.

E 2

4.

I sells all sorts of merchandize, and plenty in a small way,
My gaping jaws ne'er shut because I'm stretching of 'em all day ;
"Fresh cabbages" so green to sell I cry enough to funk ye,
And if ye won't believe, why don't, but just consult my donkey !
Ned, &c., &c., &c.

5.

Altho' I vends *purtatees*, leeks, sprats, 'errings and the h'inion,
I'm a hindependent chap as speaks, and sticks to my hopinion :
I drives my gig like any prig ; and through a crowd can shoot
    now,
And if a lie you think it—why, interrogate the brute now !
Ned, &c., &c., &c.

6.

When I'm alone, the world my own, no guv'nor by to hide me,
I gives my Sal a drive, poor gal ! oh, ain't she proud beside me ;
And as we sits, we beats to fits, the turtle doves and parrots,
For oft a bump will jolt us plump amongst the greens and carrots.
Ned, &c., &c., &c.

7.

Yet I've no frowns—for hups and downs of life is all the game, oh !
And so I vops the donkey's chops, for *some* must bear the blame, O !
There's nought annoys us sort of boys ; and every trouble sent is,
No odds to one so overdone as a costermonger's 'prentice !
Ned, &c., &c., &c.

8.

Then all you nobs, who want no jobs to set your kettles boiling,
When you repines about "hard lines" think of us coves a toiling ;
If we gets swipes to wash down tripes for once a week, a feast
    'tis,
And if you judge what I says "fudge"—My donkey here no
    beast is !

Neddy, come up—Ned, gee vo !
Ned, gee up—Gee vo !

" Who'll Sing a Song? "

Air—" Fanny Gray."

1.

" Who'll sing a song ?   We must have one !
  To help our party through,
I'm sure you will, Miss Jinkinson,
  You've always something new ! "
" Oh, say not so !   Indeed I've not ! "
  " Then give us one that's old."
" I wish I could, but I have got
  So very bad a cold.
I wish I could, but I have got
  So very bad a cold."

2.

" What shall I do !   Quadrilles they've had
  And Lancers by the dozens !
The Galop they have danc'd like mad,
  And blown our country cousins !
Oblige us, Belle !   You sing so well,
  With lessons had of Grisi ! "
" I must refuse—another choose,
  My throat it is so wheezy.
I must refuse—another choose,
  My throat it is so wheezy."

3.

" Dear Sarah Jane, delight us, do,
   With something sentimental !
Your mother bids me ask, and you
   Will grant a wish parental ! "
" Oh, ma, she really is too bad !
   And I away far wish her !
She quite forgets I too have had
   A shocking cold, ah—tish—ah ! (Sneezes.)
She quite forgets I too have had
   A shocking cold—(Sneezes) ah—tish—ah ! "

4.

" Miss Bubbs, do sing an air from ' Don
   Giovanni,' or ' Clemenza ' ? "
" Oh, dear ! I can't rely upon
   A note, from influenza !
I seldom sing, too !   Am so shy !
   Besides, I've little choice,
I must deny ! "   " Miss Bubbs, do try !
   You've such a singing voice."
" I must deny ! "   " Miss Bubbs, do try !
   You've such a singing voice ! "

5.

" I'll do my best, but when I try
   To make a telling note
There always comes in company
   A something in my throat !
Stand by me, dearest Alice—do ?
   For stare will every one,
While I sing them a ballad new,
   The words by poet Bunn !
While I sing them a ballad new,
   The words by poet Bunn ! "

6.

(Bubbs sings.) *Air*—" Whilst other lips."

No other lips to me are sweet !
  No eyes have such a glance
As Frank's ! Oh, would ma let us meet,
  His own dear love—advance !
But, as she won't—when she's asleep
  'Twixt dinner and her tea,
I'll to the jasmine arbour creep,
  And he'll remember me !
And he'll remember,
  He'll remember me !

7.

Tune—" Fanny Gray."

" Brava ! brava ! bravissima!
You've charmed us all outright ;
Your notes, my dear, have thrilled each ear
With exquisite delight !
Encore ! encore ! there's one verse more,
You've moistened every eye !
If not, repeat the same so sweet
Dear Bessie Bubbs, do try !
If not, repeat the same so sweet,
Dear Bessie Bubbs, do try !"

8.

(Bubbs sings again.) *Air*—" When other hearts, &c."

  His manly bearing all must strike
  As he approaches near ;
  They tell me that his form is like
  Th' Apollo Belvedere !

His brow will match the morning's break,
His teeth the pearls of sea!
But I must for the arbour make,
As he'll remember me!
As he'll remember,
He'll remember me!

9.

Tune—" Fanny Gray."

" Now, Mr. Priggs, the piano touch,
And sing a comic song!
There's nothing that will please so much,
And you've a list so strong!
The girls are longing, I'll be bound,
To hear some fun from you,
So something pitch like ' Bobbing round,'
Or " Hoop de dooden do!"
So something pitch like ' Bobbing round,'
Or ' Hoop de dooden do!' "

10.

(Priggs sings.) *Air*—" Gentle Zitella."

Sweet Isabella!
Come to me, dear,
Think a poor *feller*,
Waits for thee here,
Shiv'ring with wet, love,
Come to me soon.
Gazing I get, love,
Sick of the moon!
Sweet Isabella,
Come to me, dear!
Think a poor *feller*
Waits for thee here.

11.

(Priggs sings.) *Tune*—" Fanny Gray."

She comes, she comes ! Let no one sing,
E'en comic songs are slow,
When most would fly in galops by
On light fantastic toe.
A few might laugh, but more would chaff,
While many a one all through
The night would twirl his favourite girl
In " Hoop de dooden do ! "
The night would twirl his favourite girl
In " Hoop de dooden do ! "

Limited Liability.

Air—" Bundle of Truths," or " Barney Bodkin."

1.

Golden age has come at last,
    Snatch the moments as they fly !
All can make a fortune fast !
    Safely too—I'll tell you why,
Companies your purse can fill—
    See the lists and have your shy !
For they now have pass'd the Bill
    Limiting liability !

Then go, go, go ahead !
    Gulls and gudgeons must be bled.
Nought takes too like diddle 'em do,
    Now the risk is limited.

2.

Bless the House of Commons' nobs,
    Limiting a losing game !
They have given a lift to jobs
    Far too numerous to name.
Here's the last new company—
    Try a chance and do not fear !
'Tis to break monopoly
    By an ope n trade in beer !
        Then go, go, go ahead ! &c.

3.

Here's a lot of specs for all
   Pockets, whether small or big.
Shares apply for—pay the call—
   Heedless who the markets rig!
Here's a company by steam
   Shirts to wash or pantaloons—
Here is one for milk and cream,
   Dairy pork, the best of boons.
            So go, go, go ahead! &c.

4.

Here are mines of lead and tin
   Promising rich dividends—
Yet there's none can stand to win
   But the chap who money spends!
Gold mines too—and silver set
   Glistening to all around—
So if rich you cannot get
   On the earth—try underground!
            And go, go, go ahead! &c.

5.

Nought entices like a scheme!
   No one need a business learn!
Companies to "Hatch by Steam"
   Pledge for all a quick return.
"Paper made of Niggers' wool,"
   Or a "Railway to the Moon"
Will if calls are paid in full
   Make your fortune precious soon!
            Then go, go, go ahead! &c.

6.

" Telegraphs " from Pole to Pole
  May a sinking income prop,
If good luck will keep the whole
  Like a *bubble* on the top !
" Deep Sea Fishing "—ne'er too deep
  For a crafty jobber's wish :
Whilst limited secure will keep
  Tempting one to further fish.
            So go, go, go ahead ! &c.

7.

Companies to well insure
  Bread that none adulterate—
When the staff of life is pure,
  Is it not a wholesome state ?
Guarantees 'gainst accident
  As the locomotive goes,
Compensate to full extent
  For a broken leg or nose.
            Then go, go, go ahead ! &c.

8.

Here's a matrimonial spec !
  Company to keep a wife !
Try your lucky—for 'tis neck
  Or nothing when you pair for life.
Limited now is all the go,
  Subject fit for prose or song—
Ev'ry thing limited is you know
  But law costs or woman's tongue !
            So go, go, go ahead ! &c.

9.

" Life Assurance " by the score,
  Saving money few can make !
That's to say—when one's no more—
  They will pay and no mistake !
All are " Indisputable "—
  Don't you wish that you may get it ?
Nothing is immutable,
  When a law-suit can upset it.
            Then go, go, go ahead ! &c.

10.

Limited !   Ah, that's the thing !
  Check to artful dodgers' pranks—
Would they'd thought of limiting
  Ere I'd trusted " British Banks."
Limiting then was never seen,
  All was " diddle 'em di " and " do "—
I thought my eye contain'd no *green*,
  But my whole complexion's *blue !*
    Then go, go, go ahead,
      Gulls and gudgeons must be bled,
    So I fear 'tis " all my eye,"
      Limiting liability.

They are all Washing.

(On Providing Baths and Wash-houses for the Poor.)

Tune—"They are a' Noddin."

1.

They are all washing,
Wash, wash, washing,
They are all washing, at baths for the poor.
See, see, how they run !
Full late for the fun—
Mrs. Brown toddles down
With ev'ry little Brown.

And they're all washing,
Wash, wash, washing,
They are all washing at baths for the poor.

2.

By dozens they sally
From court, lane, and alley,
Seeking a dip in the baths for the poor.
Oh, there can't be offence
At the public expense—
So they strip for their skip
In the general dip.
      And they're all washing, &c.

3.

Soon, soon, will it prove
A very good move—
Washing-house building, and baths for the poor,
Did you ever see the like !
There's Paddy, and Mike,
And Jemmy, and Jack,
A scrubbing o' the back.
                        And they're all washing, &c.

4.

Oh, lawk ! what a sight,
By day and by night,
To see them all plunge in baths for the poor.
There are dustmen and dray
A smoking of their clay,
And reposing they seem
As they lounge upon the stream,
                        And they're all washing, &c.

5.

Mrs. Grub has her tea,
The best of Bohea,
Her evening dish at the baths for the poor
But her draught is nigh done
Ere she hears her high son (Hyson)
Near to her tumble in
To renovate his skin.
                        And they're all washing, &c.

6.

Mrs. Squibb feels alarms
To see such arms
Display'd o'er the top of baths for the poor,
In vain does she cry,
And kick up a splash—
A few may say fie!
But the country says " Wash."
            So they're all washing, &c.

7.

Haste, haste, come and see
What a comical spree
Is now going on at baths for the poor—
There fat ones and thin
Are floundering in,
While tall ones and short
Make cleanliness a sport.
            And they're all washing, &c.

8.

'Twas a step in the right
Direction quite,
Giving a chance of washing to the poor—
Now ev'ry one hath
A comfortable bath—
Where each, like his "*bett'rers*,"
Can wash all et ceteras.
            And they're all washing, &c.

9.

This London town
Is the best I own
To get polish'd off at baths for the poor.
Though ever in a fog,
You may wander *incog.*
To wash one is sent
By Act of Parliament,
So they're all washing, &c.

10.

I'm quite perplex'd
To think what next
Will follow on to the baths for the poor—
Some strange new scheme
Will be the theme—
But nought like a *moat*
Can keep the world afloat.
And they're all washing, &c.

11.

They are all washing,
Wash, wash, washing—
They are all washing at baths for the poor.
If measures be good
Let's have 'em in a *flood.*
So friends never throw
Cold water on them, Oh!
Yet they're all washing,
Wash, wash, washing,
They are all washing at baths for the poor.

F

A Dream at Madame Tussaud's.

Air—" I dreamt I dwelt in Marble Halls."

1.

I dreamt, when I slept at Madame Tussaud's,
    Of nobbies of every degree,
Of snobbies as well in their holiday clothes,
    Who all for a *bob* you may see.
I saw the rum lot in the dead of the night
    Come forth like bees in swarms !
And comical rigs they brought to light
    In their spermaceti forms.

2.

I saw the great Napoleon shake
    A toe with the good Mrs. Fry ;
How Louis Philippe in his funk did not take
    Snuff to his nose, but his eye.
I saw how Queen Bess made Guinness's stout
    Down Father Matthew flow ;
And Billy the Fourth, with grog cold without,
    Sang, "The Bay of Biscay, O !"

3.

I saw Prince Blucher smoking his clay
    Along with Cardinal Wiseman ;
While Dan. O'Connell the bagpipes did play
    To John of Gaunt the big size-man.
And then Paganini, with fiddle and stick,
    Made Louis Napoleon dance ;
While Harry the Eighth sang out, " Kiss me quick,"
    To Joan of Arc of France !

4.

I saw Dicky Cobden, of speech unadorn'd,
  Set to,—with a lord of the soil !
I twigg'd too the " Rail King " on whom subjects fawn'd
  Get kicks for his tricks and his spoil.
And as the great Lights together did mix,
  " *Long fours* " and " short sixes "—the game
In wax, as in flesh and bones, seem'd that six
  Or a half dozen were just the same.

5.

In the chamber of horrors an Auth'ress stood
  Studying by *Rush*-light phrenology ;
Intent upon Manning—Greenacre—and Goode !
  Some women are past all apology !
When all of a sudden mid terrible noise
  A Buffer—with a screech—
Stood forth and cried out, " Attention, my boys,
  John Bright will make you a speech ! "

6.

But then Johnny Russell would " thimble rig " have,
  Whilst Palmerston called for " Aunt Sally ;"
And Malb'rough, Wellington, Nelson so brave !
  Pio Nono and Sir Walter Raleigh,
With Paul Pry and John Knox for " knock'em downs " spake,
  And just as fighting began,
In came Mother Tussaud, when I did awake,
  And took to my heels—and ran.

Mrs. Codlings.

Tune—" Mrs. Waddle was a Widow."

1.

Mrs. Codlings lived at Ryde
 And she kept a boarding school—
Of all Academies the pride!
 For there they learnt the rule
To slide into a curtsey, and
 A wriggling gait—just so!
Oh! didn't Mother Codlings' band
 Make a pretty show—
  As two, two, two,
   Two, two, two,
 A bathing they did go!

(*Spoken.*) Now, girls, we begin our *dips* for the season, and I beg you won't make *light* of them. If you look into the sea, observe how the little fish dance with the big *swells*—but don't follow so bad an example—don't look over the sea, and then you can't see any thing on the sea you ought not to see. Jemima Caroline, take the arm of Miss Weathercock, and fall in—keep step Miss Walker. "I love order," as my ever to be lamented Codlings used to say, it *looks so domesticated;* and I promised your *dear* parents to conduct every thing in a family way.

> So two, two, two,
> Two, two, two,
> A bathing they did go.

2.

> Machines are reach'd and in they're put,
>   Half dozens cramm'd in each—
> To tell the rigs when doors were shut
>   Defies the parts of speech—
> And when they frisk it merrily
>   Within the water cool,
> Oh, isn't it a jolly spree
>   For Mother Codlings' school!
>   As two, two two,
>   Two, two, two,
>   A bathing they did go!

(*Spoken.*) Oh, isn't it cha-ar-ar-ming!—not at all cold—not in the least—quite wa-arm—any thing but co-old. Well, and if the water hasn't got in at one ear and won't come out of the other! Clara Brown come off the steps! Shivering, too, like a mummy just unwound—what are you afraid of, I should like to know! Got no bathing dress, ma'am. Then get into Arabella Bounce's, big enough for both of you! Come down, I say; look at me, mastering the waves like a man-of-war—does what I like with them—goes where I like—quite at home in the water!

> So two, two, two,
> Two, two, two,
> A bathing they did go.

3.

A souse from brawny bather's arms,
 And then another dip—
And then in rings, with clenching palms,
 The pretty creatures skip.
In vain does Mother Codlings try
 To make them mind her wishes,
Such *ducks* will bring the loungers by,
 And scare the little *fishes*.
  As two, two, two,
   Two, two, two,
 A bathing they did go.

Spoken. Bless me, bathing woman, what's that? Oh! it's only a dirty *buoy*, marm! I hope he'll keep his distance, then! most improper to put him there! There's a smack! A what, Miss Jenkins? I'm astonished. Don't let me hear such words again.

(Bathing woman interferes.) The Young Lady, marm, is mistaken. It's only a " billy-boy,"—one of yer north country crafts, marm! Plenty on 'em here, sometimes.

(Mrs C.) Time to be off, girls! And if there is'nt that horrid Capt. Weatherley blowing this way like a grampus! with his Crimean beard too, and his Mount St. Bernard pups—Shouldn't bring such things into the water!

  So, two, two, two,
   Two, two, two,
 A bathing they did go.

4.

Fast from the horrid monster then,
 The girls are forced to fly ;
And how they went, or where and when,
Dame Codlings could not spy.

Retreat full soon became a rout,
　The like was never seen !
And in the while some stupid lout
　Had wheel'd off her machine !
　　When two, two, two,
　　　Two, two, two,
　A bathing they did go.

(*Spoken.*) I think, my dear sir, you've made a slight mistake.
Holloa ! who's there ?—can't come in I say, can't, 'pon my word !
What do you want ?　These are the gentlemen's machines, old
gal ! Old gal, indeed ! I'm Mrs. Codlings, of Sea View Academy.
Very likely, but you must put out to sea again, and cruise in
another direction.　You've lost your reckoning, old gal.　Well !
if this isn't enough to make one —— No, I won't say it !—No !
but I'll sit on yonder rock mistress of all I survey ; or, as Shakes-
pere has it, like " patience on a monument."　All very fine !—
but patience is very trying sometimes, and if this isn't a *cold*
water cure, I don't know what is !

　　So two, two, two,
　　　Two, two, two,
　A bathing they did go !

5.

" Good lack ! " cried Mrs. Codlings, " Sure
　Could Codlings, love, but spy
Me shivering from door to door,
　He'd freely pipe his eye !
I'm come to grief ! for I've no thought
　Where my machine can be.
So no more bathing I'll be caught,
　It puts one all at sea !
　　As two, two, two,
　　　Two, two, two,
　A bathing we do go."

Spoken. Well, I begin to think I'm left to bewail—yes, very like a whale ! More like a disappointed mermaid with nothing to sit on ; but I see how it is, I am a lost, unprotected female—so I'll *flounder* ashore with ev'ry one eyeing me as a queer fish—why ! there's a mob on the beach ! Oh ! if Codlings were to see his good old " *soul* " (sole) taken for a common " *plaice*," and be bundled home any how, wouldn't he fret just ; it's enough to make one *crab*-bed ! but it's the last time I'll go sea bathing : for it's plain to me I am no *dab* at it !

As two, two, two,
Two, two, two,
A bathing they did go.

6.

Now parents, who the female mind
In innocence would rear,
A watering place the place you'll find
To teach the young idea !
And who would strain to get a plain
Instruction at the sea,
Will find Dame Codlings in the *main*
A good Academy.
For two, two, two,
Two, two, two,
A bathing they do go.

Grandmother.

Tune—" My Grandfather was a most wonderful Man."

1.

My grandmother was a remarkable dame,
Whatever went wrong she was never to blame;
Whilst but a girl and a Miss in her teens
She was well up to snuff, to chaff, and to beans—
She knew every thing much better than others—
Would punish the youngsters, both sisters and brothers.

SPOKEN. Punish! I believe you, she could punish a *leetle* bit
—and couldn't the old lady read the riot act when she had the
opportunity! Grandfather knew this well enough, so he was a
very quiet going sort of old customer. He'd known what it was
to put *her* "monkey up," as she used to call it—Grandmother
pull'd the old geutleman's nose clean out of joint in early life, and
he never could follow it arterwards.

What a pity it is she lives only in name,
For grandmother was an astonishing dame—
My grandmother was an astonishing dame!

2.

The rest of the family heads all the while
Ne'er ventur'd to meddle with grandmother's bile;
For when her old monkey got up to the crown,
The devil a bit would the rascal come down!
So the only safe cure was to let it alone—
For strong was her voice, and uncommon the tone.

SPOKEN.   Voice! I believe you, grandmother had something
like a voice! Catalani, you know, crack'd one of your grand
chimney glasses with *her* voice, but grandmother beat her all to
fits—she did!—she blew the pebbles clean out of grandfather's
spectacles once, and it so injur'd the old gentleman's sight, that
she got on the blind side of him ever afterwards—she knew very
well what she was a doing of !

What a pity it is, then, she lives but in name,
For grandmother was a remarkable dame—
My grandmother was a most wonderful dame.

3.

She'd seen such queer sights as no others had seen;
Had been in such places no others had been;
What any one knew, why grandmother knew more—
In short the old gal was too often a bore.
In curing distempers the world she'd surprise,
And bother the dons of St. George's or Guy's.

SPOKEN.   Ah, she was a marvellous doctor! such a hand at a
sore, too! Holloway's ointment was a fool to grandmother's! she
cur'd the worst wound uncle ever had on his wooden leg with
" turpentine and bees' wax "—she did! Her very look was a dose

for you—it went through you at once, and you never came a second
time for "the mixture as before." She understood egotism,
magnetism, gargarism, heroism, organism, *boy*ism, *gal*vanism,
and rheumatism! Astrology, pathology, geology, pharmacology,
physiology, anthropology, botonology, myology, phythology,
biology, zoology, nosology, and every other sort of ology!

What a pity it is, then, she lives but in name,
For my grandmother was an astonishing dame—
My grandmother was a most wonderful dame.

4.

She knew why some people were fat and some thin,
Could tell when a babby had swallowed a pin!
Could twig when a maiden a sweetheart had got,
And tell if a lover were jilted or not.
The cleverest folk that e'er stood on two legs,
Could never instruct the old gal to *suck eggs!*

SPOKEN.—I should think not! Nothing was new to grandmother—there was no gammoning the old lady, that you may
take my word for—and there was no sham about the old woman
neither! Grandmother wore none of your hoops and crinolines
as some ladies do, and make more spread in the world than many
grandmammas nowadays think reasonable or respectable.

What a pity it is, then, she lives but in name,
For grandmother was a most circumspect dame—
My grandmother was a most circumspect dame.

5.

Yet granny had kindness, could cover a slip,
Which oftentimes comes 'twixt the cup and the lip.
If you told her at once, and came out with it plump,
She'd fight your worst battle, and stand like a trump—
In short, she would prove then a sensible *cratur*,
And make some allowance for poor human *natur*.

SPOKEN.—Ay, poor old gal! she had some good pints about her
arter all. Only have pluck enough to *face* her—sensible old
soul—when she found it couldn't be help'd she'd hush it up and
say nothing about it.

What a pity it is, then, she lives but in name,
For grandmother was a most sensible dame—
My grandmother was a considerate dame.

6.

She's gone, poor old gal, and 'twould puzzle my wits
To tell all her rigs in her comical fits—
If it wouldn't fatigue you, 'twould me, so I can't,
'Tis enough that the " *oldest known inhabitant* "
Was outdone by her,—so I'm sure you'll agree,
No woman was ever so knowing as she!

What a pity it is, then, she lives but in name,
For grandmother was a most wonderful dame—
My grandmother was an astonishing dame!

Volunteers.

Tune—"Malbrook."

1.

Oh ! dear, what means this commotion !
Are the French 'bout crossing the ocean ?
There's some seem to scoff at the notion—
      But we raise volunteers !
      Our fighting men are few,
      And it might be a *"reg'lar do !"*
But should old Parlez vous Français
Come over to lead us a dance, say,
Should we relish the circumstance, eh !
      Without our volunteers ?

2.

Mountsier may envy our shore now !
To wipe away an old score now,
And which he'd have done long before now !
      But for our volunteers—
      For know, my lads, of old
      Our volunteers so bold
Kept enemies clear from our island,
And they never put foot upon dry land—
And they can't whilst a Briton says, " My land
      Shall have its volunteers ! "

3.

Then should our neighbours come over
To take up snug quarters at Dover !
Or for a good slice of our clover—
        They'll find our volunteers
        Across the channel chops
        Can raise on Kentish tops
A hop—they don't commonly grow there,
But once let an enemy go there—
He'll dance it ; and never more show there
        To British volunteers.

4.

Enlisting for men we don't now care,
And pressing to fight is not now fair,
John " Whop Straw" would soon leave his ploughshare
        To join the volunteers !
        What he ! a son of the soil,
        And let a foreigner spoil
His home—go and spout, Dickey Cobden,
And skulk off behind your own hob when
Attack'd—while we settle the job, then,
        Like British volunteers !

5.

See Doughey, the baker, in blue, sir,
His temper not *crusty* — but true, sir,
To his country obeys the tattoo, sir,
        Of British volunteers !
        The tinman leaves his kettle
        To join Britannia *mettle !*
No " parsley bed " chap is the grocer !
The cellarman no more is *low,* sir !
The watchmaker's *main spring's* not slow, sir,
        To march with volunteers !

6.

For marrow bones little relief now,
To the tune of " England's Roast Beef " now
They march—but our butcher's no grief now
      To be a volunteer—
      He's a martial looking chap !
      Jack Stiles, who keeps the tap
Of the " King's " or " Queen's Head," or the " Crown," sir,
Sings out, and its sung through each town, sir !
" Old England can ne'er be done *Brown*, sir,
      Whilst she has volunteers ! "

7.

No *longer* Joe Wiggins—nor *shorter*
Cuts hair ; and he's left his old quarter.
Our chymist, with pestle and mortar,
      Is now a volunteer !
      Our barber with his pole
      There's no one can control !
And tho' his old woman keeps chiding
He's off in the movement a striding !
The tanner, so well up to *hiding*,
      Is, too, a volunteer !

8.

Should foes think of seeking our shore now,
Our cannons will prove a great *bore* now !
And Britons don't slumber and snore now
      In want of volunteers—
      The British Lion's roar
      All enemies can floor !
When rous'd, and his mane he's a shaking,
He'll set ev'ry foreigner quaking,
Whilst thousands their rifles are taking
      Like gallant volunteers !

9.

Huzza! for the Queen, and may she long
Reign o'er us, and stick as she be long
With subjects a happy and free throng,
   And trusty volunteers!
   Then should across the deep
   Some sly armada creep!
Our shores and our homes all at stake then!
John Bull will be found wide awake then,
Oh! where is the harm we can take then
   With gallant volunteers?

EDWARD WEST, PRINTER, 97, NEWGATE STREET, LONDON.

www.ingramcontent.com/pod-product-compliance
Lightning Source LLC
Chambersburg PA
CBHW081519040426
42447CB00013B/3269